HAL•LEONARD
INSTRUMENTAL
PLAY-ALONG

AUDIO
ACCESS
INCLUDED

PLAYBACK+
Speed • Pitch • Balance • Loop

THE GREATEST SHOWMAN

T0078621

Audio Arrangements by Peter Deneff

To access audio visit:
www.halleonard.com/mylibrary

6473-5966-9094-9886

ISBN 978-1-5400-2849-5

HAL•LEONARD®

7777 W. BLUEMOUND RD. P.O. BOX 13819 MILWAUKEE, WI 53213

In Australia Contact:
Hal Leonard Australia Pty. Ltd.
4 Lentara Court
Cheltenham, Victoria, 3192 Australia
Email: ausadmin@halleonard.com.au

Visit Hal Leonard Online at
www.halleonard.com

COME ALIVE

CELLO

Words and Music by BENJ PASEK
and JUSTIN PAUL

FROM NOW ON

CELLO

Words and Music by BENJ PASEK
and JUSTIN PAUL

THE GREATEST SHOW

CELLO

Words and Music by BENJ PASEK,
JUSTIN PAUL and RYAN LEWIS

A MILLION DREAMS

CELLO

Words and Music by BENJ PASEK
and JUSTIN PAUL

NEVER ENOUGH

CELLO

Words and Music by BENJ PASEK
and JUSTIN PAUL

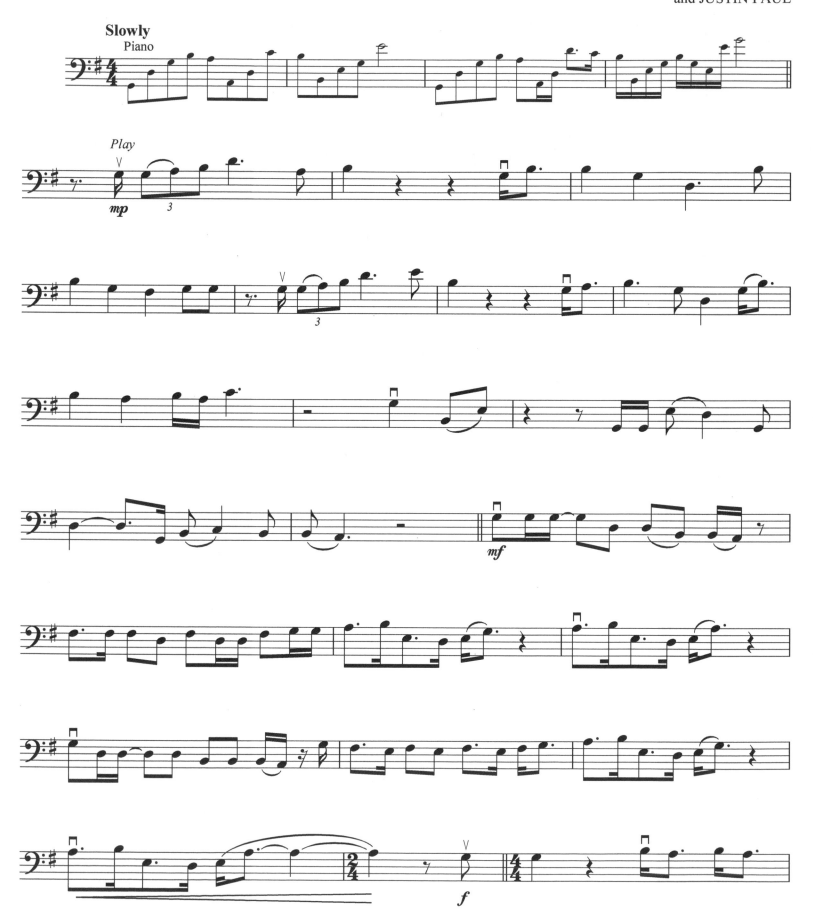

THE OTHER SIDE

CELLO

Words and Music by BENJ PASEK
and JUSTIN PAUL

REWRITE THE STARS

CELLO

Words and Music by BENJ PASEK
and JUSTIN PAUL

THIS IS ME

CELLO

Words and Music by BENJ PASEK
and JUSTIN PAUL

TIGHTROPE

CELLO

Words and Music by BENJ PASEK
and JUSTIN PAUL